Colors of
FRANCE

written and illustrated by Helen Byers

Carolrhoda Books, Inc. / Minneapolis

To the memory of my grandmother, Clara Laura Primm (de la Pryme) Byers, who knew China but not this land of her ancestors; and to the entire family of Denis Le Cren, who brought France to life for me.

With special thanks to Richard Godden and Rhian Hughes, for the pigeonnier; and to Tomos and Mabli, for trying to lift the dolmen.

This book is available in two editions:
Library binding by Carolrhoda Books, Inc., a division of Lerner Publishing Group
Soft cover by First Avenue Editions, an imprint of Lerner Publishing Group
241 First Avenue North
Minneapolis, MN 55401 U.S.A.

Website address: www.lernerbooks.com

Library of Congress Cataloging-in-Publication Data

Byers, Helen.
    Colors of France / written and illustrated by Helen Byers.
      p.   cm. — (Colors of the world)
    Includes index.
    ISBN: 1–57505–514–7 (lib. bdg. : alk. paper)
    ISBN: 1–57505–565–1 (pbk. : alk. paper)
    1. France—Juvenile literature. 2. Colors, Words for—Juvenile literature.
  [1. France. 2. Color.] I. Title. II. Series.
  DC17 .B96 2002
  944—dc21   2001001137

Manufactured in the United States of America
1 2 3 4 5 6 – JR – 07 06 05 04 03 02

England · English Channel · FLANDERS · BELGIUM · GERMANY · PICARDY · LUXEMBOURG · Paris · LORRAINE · NORMANDY · Versailles · ALSACE · BRITTANY · Seine River · ATLANTIC OCEAN · Loire River · FRANCE · SWITZERLAND · ITALY · Rhône River · A L P S · Grasse · PROVENCE · Côte d'Azur · MONACO · ANDORRA · Camargue · CORSICA · PYRENNEES · MEDITERRANEAN SEA · SPAIN

Introduction

France is a land where colorful history mixes with exciting modern life. Paris, the capital, is called the City of Light. Some people say it is the most exciting city in the world. France is one of the biggest countries in Europe. Yet it is not quite as big as the state of Texas. If you squint, a map of France looks like a six-pointed star or a starfish. France shares borders with Belgium, Luxembourg, Germany, Switzerland, Italy, Monaco, Andorra, and Spain. The official language of France is French. Arabic, Basque, Breton, and Flemish are also spoken in parts of France.

3

White

Blanc (BLAHN)

White horses run wild on the Camargue (kah-MAHRG). The Camargue is a saltwater marsh where the Rhône River meets the Mediterranean Sea. Wading birds—white egrets, ibises, and flamingos—live in its shallow waters and grasses. People harvest rice and sea salt along parts of the shore.

The Camargue horse is an ancient breed. It is related to horses ridden in the south of France thousands of years ago. When Camargue horses are born, they have brown coats. Their coats turn white by the time they are five years old.

French cowboys ride some of the Camargue horses. The cowboys are called *gardiens* (gahr-dee-EH), which means "caretakers."

6

Lavender

Lavande (lah-VAHND)

In the fields of Provence, **lavender** flowers perfume the wind. They are the blossoms of an herb called lavender. The flower buds look like grains of pale purple rice on a long, stiff stem.

In the 1600s, people in the town of Grasse discovered lavender could scent their gloves. They began to use lavender to make perfume. Grasse became the perfume-making capital of the world. People all over the world still buy perfumes made from French lavender—as well as from French lilies, roses, and other flowers and herbs. French lavender is also used to make soap, scented candles, and insect repellent.

Every summer, when the lavender blooms, fields are covered in strips of purple. People in the towns and villages of Provence hold festivals to celebrate.

Gold

Or (OR)

Nearly everything inside the Palace of Versailles is painted with pure **gold.** Gold was the favorite color of King Louis XIV. The most famous room in Versailles is the Hall of Mirrors, where Louis held fancy parties. The gold chamber is almost as long as a football field. When the sun sets, golden light gleams through the tall windows on one side of the hall. The light is reflected in tall mirrors on the other side.

Louis XIV ruled France from 1643 to 1715—longer than any other king, emperor, or president. He believed that God had given him the right to rule. In fact, he thought he was the most important ruler in the universe next to God. Louis paid artists, writers, musicians, and architects to create great works. In this way, he believed that he cast the light of knowledge upon his subjects. So Louis XIV was called the Sun King. The sun and the sunflower became his emblems.

9

Red

Rouge (ROOZH)

Red poppies bloom on the old battlefields of northern France. There is a legend that Genghis Khan brought the first white poppy from China. He was a great Mongolian ruler in the 1200s. According to the story, white poppies that grew from his seeds turned red after battle.

In World War I, over a million soldiers died in northern France. The fields were covered with barbed wire and mud. Trenches cut across them. After the war, the wild red poppy was one of the few plants that would grow on the battlefields.

Poppies now carpet the fields in scarlet. Nearby, rows and rows of white crosses fill military cemeteries. The red poppy has become a symbol of remembrance.

11

Green

Vert (VEHR)

In formal French gardens, **green** trees and shrubs are planted in precise patterns. They are closely clipped into fancy shapes. The trees and shrubs often surround a fountain, pool, or statue. Sometimes they are planted and clipped to form a maze. In a maze, people who stroll through the garden could get lost!

Formal gardens are often planted around castles called *châteaux* (sha-TOH). Many châteaux were built in the Loire Valley by aristocrats nearly four hundred years ago. There are also formal gardens in the many parks of Paris and of other cities and towns. Surrounded by beautiful greenery, people lounge, read, and walk from spring to winter.

13

Gray

Gris (GREE)

A **gray** stone monster on the cathedral of Notre Dame leers down at people on the street. Another glares up the river toward the Eiffel Tower. These stone monsters are called chimeras (kee-MIR-uhz). Notre Dame's chimeras look like the one in an ancient Greek myth—a monster that is part goat, part lion, and part dragon. Between the church's two towers you might spy some gentler stone creatures, such as monkeys, birds, and elephants. But you might be worried by the gargoyles. These hideous demons, monsters, and human forms lean out from the sides of the cathedral. Their mouths serve as rainspouts, spewing water when it rains!

The cathedral of Notre Dame stands on a small island in the Seine River in the middle of Paris. It was begun in the 1100s and took two hundred years to build. Outside, its high walls are supported by gigantic arches called flying buttresses. Stone decorations are carved like lace. Inside, arched ceilings reach to the sky, and huge stained-glass windows glow. In 1833, Victor Hugo wrote his famous novel, *The Hunchback of Notre Dame*, about a lonely bell ringer living in the cathedral's towers.

Orange

Orange (oh-RAHNZH)

In many areas of France, rooftops are made of **orange** clay tiles. In the north, in Flanders and Picardy, the tiles are flat. The roofs are steeply slanted to let rainwater run off. In the south, where there is less rain, the slope of roofs is less steep. There, the clay tiles are curved. In Provence, many rooftops are steepest on the north side. This design protects the houses from the sharp northern wind called the Mistral. The rooftops are flatter on the south side. On the south side, there are windows for letting in the soft warm breezes of the Mediterranean.

18

Blue

Bleu (BLUH)

On the warm shores of the Mediterranean Sea, the **blue** waters of the Côte d'Azur draw crowds of vacationers. The English word "azure," borrowed from French, is another name for this brilliant shade of blue.

The other seashores of France do not have beaches like the Côte d'Azur. On the coasts of Brittany, there are granite boulders as big as houses. On the shores of Normandy, there are high, chalky cliffs.

Jacques Cousteau lived on the Côte d'Azur. He was fascinated by the sea. Cousteau became a great underwater explorer. He traveled the world's oceans on his ship *Calypso*. Cousteau invented the aqua-lung and the undersea laboratory. In dozens of movies and TV shows, Cousteau showed the deep blue oceans to viewers around the world.

Black

Noir (NWAHR)

In many parts of France, people wear **black.** It is both stylish and traditional. For weddings, funerals, and festivals in Brittany, some men wear traditional black hats and jackets. Some women and girls wear black jackets and dark skirts. They also wear hand-made lace collars and lace caps called *coiffes* (KWAHF). The collar and coiffe are so stiffly starched that they stand up—or out. Each town in Brittany has its own special style of coiffe.

The people of Brittany share history with people in Great Britain. Along with French, they speak Breton—a language related to Welsh. They even play the bagpipes.

Yellow

Jaune (ZHOHN)

The leader of the Tour de France wears a **yellow** jersey. This bicycle race is held every summer in France. About a month before the race, the International Cycling Union invites about 20 of the best teams from different countries to take part. Each team has nine riders. The racecourse is one huge circle through the French countryside. The course is over two thousand miles long. The cyclists spend three weeks competing. They race on flat land, past fields of sunflowers. They race through villages and towns. And they race up and down mountain roads in the Alps and the Pyrenees.

In the last leg of the race, the cyclists ride up the most famous street in Paris—the Champs-Elysées (SHAWZ-el-ee-ZAY)—and under the Arc de Triomphe. The Arc de Triomphe, the "arch of triumph," is the world's largest victory arch.

Index